The Homeschooler's

High School Journal

$$A = \pi r^2$$
$$C = 2\pi r^2$$

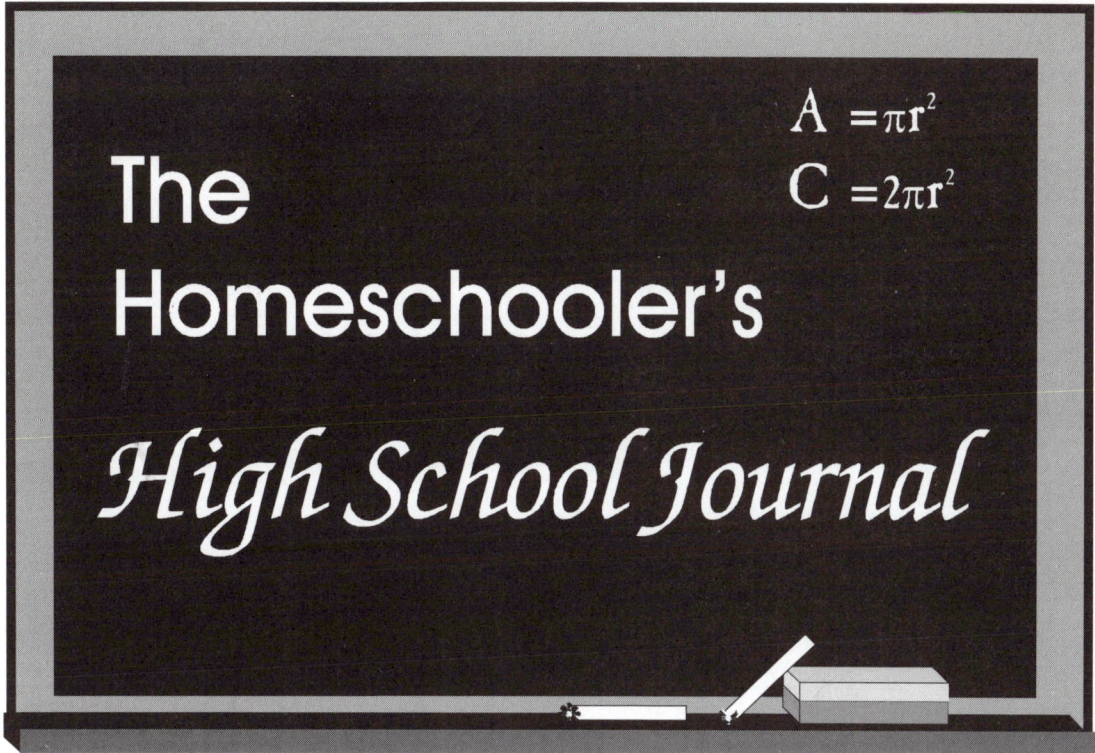

Name of School: _____

Address: _____

_____

Telephone Number (_____) _____ School Year: _____

Student's Name: _____

Teacher's Name: _____

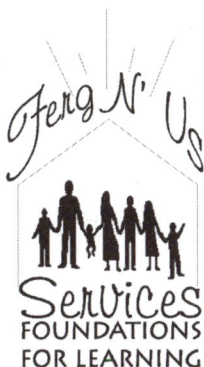

Ferg N' Us

Services
FOUNDATIONS
FOR LEARNING

ISBN 0-9785413-1-6

9 780978 541316

The Homeschooler's High School Journal Instructions

Homeschooling may be new to you and keeping a log or journal may be required by your state. There are many different styles of teaching so we have designed The Homeschooler's High School Journal to accommodate some of these differences. We encourage new homeschoolers to experiment with different types of schooling methods. Perhaps you will find, as we did, that combinations of methods work well.

	1 Subject _Bible_	2 Subject _Math_	3 Subject _History_	5 Subject _For. Lang._
S M T W T F S Date /	Chapter #1 - Priceless Woman the Titus II Quiet time devotions	Algebra 1 - pp. 115, 116 Study for test	Timeline using World History Dates. Read about Customs and Manners Bible Lands. pp. 28 - 40 Streams of Civilizations	Chapter #3 Destinas

	3 Subject _English_	4 Subject _Art_	7 Subject _Business_	1 Subject _Bible_
S M T W T F S Date /	Read Biography of Abigal Adams Dictation from Proverbs 31. Read and outline the Writing process from Writer Inc.	Teaching Art to younger students, Sketching a self-portrait.	Data entry filing filling address processing check deposits.	List the Godly attributes of Abigal Adams.

Subject #	Time in Quarter-hours	Weekly Total
1		3:15
3		2:45
4		4:30
5		3:45
6		3:00

To keep track of hours spent on a subject, just fill in a circle for each hour completed. The hours circles are divided into 15 minute segments. At the end of each week, add up the number of hours you have spent on each subject and write the totals in the box under the heading "Weekly Total".

Instructions for use of the Daily Attendance, Subjects and Grades:

The design of the Homeschooler's High School is for overall compatibility between sections. Therefore, as you will notice on the daily attendance page, there are spaces marked #1, #2, #3, etc. Those spaces are to assign individual subjects, i.e. English, mathematics, science, with a number to be used each quarter of the school year. The same numbered subject may be used on each individual log space in the daily planner, and may also be used in the Hours Completed chart each week. Thus completing a unified system throughout the school year. As electives change from quarter to quarter the subject numbers may be changed also. Daily Grades may be averaged every five days to give an overall view of the student's progress throughout the quarter (See example below).

A NOTE on Grades:

In the high school years it is not absolutely necessary to issue grades. Many colleges have been known to accept students with transcripts and/or SAT/ACT scores, but this is not the norm. (The high moral character and willingness to serve and learn has been a great contributing factor in allowing more home educated students to attend higher learning facilities without grade averages.) If the student intends to someday attend a higher education institution, practice in receiving a grade, as an evaluation, can be useful tools.

Date	Attendance	Bible	Math	English	History	Foreign Language	Creative Arts	Business	Science	Music	Practical Art
		1	2	3	4	5	6	7	8	9	10
9/8	1	95	92	90	96				88		
9/9	2	92	88	82						98	90
9/10	3		90		95				80	100	
9/11	4	98	86				90	92			
9/12	5	98	92			82			87		
GRADE AVERAGE		96	90	86	96	82	90	92	85	99	90

We hope and pray your high school years are fruitful and filled with growth in character and wisdom as you make your decisions for your future. We thank you for your purchase of The Homeschooler's High School Journal and hope that it will serve you well.

God Bless,
The Ferguson's

Linear Schedule of Home Schooling Events

DATE	JULY	AUGUST	SEPTEMBER	OCTOBER	NOVEMBER	DECEMBER
1						
2						
3						
4						
5						
6						
7						
8						
9						
10						
11						
12						
13						
14						
15						
16						
17						
18						
19						
20						
21						
22						
23						
24						
25						
26						
27						
28						
29						
30						
31	JULY	AUGUST		OCTOBER		DECEMBER

Linear Schedule of Home Schooling Events

JANUARY	FEBRUARY	MARCH	APRIL	MAY	JUNE	DATE
						1
						2
						3
						4
						5
						6
						7
						8
						9
						10
						11
						12
						13
						14
						15
						16
						17
						18
						19
						20
						21
						22
						23
						24
						25
						26
						27
						28
						29
						30
						31

2010 - 2011 School Year

JULY – 2010

SUN	MON	TUES	WED	THUR	FRI	SAT
				1	2	3
4	5	6	7	8	9	10
11	12	13	14	15	16	17
18	19	20	21	22	23	24
25	26	27	28	29	30	31

JANUARY – 2011

SUN	MON	TUES	WED	THUR	FRI	SAT
						1
2	3	4	5	6	7	8
9	10	11	12	13	14	15
16	17	18	19	20	21	22
23/30	24/31	25	26	27	28	29

AUGUST – 2010

SUN	MON	TUES	WED	THUR	FRI	SAT
1	2	3	4	5	6	7
8	9	10	11	12	13	14
15	16	17	18	19	20	21
22	23	24	25	26	27	28
29	30	31				

FEBRUARY – 2011

SUN	MON	TUES	WED	THUR	FRI	SAT
		1	2	3	4	5
6	7	8	9	10	11	12
13	14	15	16	17	18	19
20	21	22	23	24	25	26
27	28					

SEPTEMBER– 2010

SUN	MON	TUES	WED	THUR	FRI	SAT
			1	2	3	4
5	6	7	8	9	10	11
12	13	14	15	16	17	18
19	20	21	22	23	24	25
26	27	28	29	30		

MARCH – 2011

SUN	MON	TUES	WED	THUR	FRI	SAT
		1	2	3	4	5
6	7	8	9	10	11	12
13	14	15	16	17	18	19
20	21	22	23	24	25	26
27	28	29	30	31		

OCTOBER – 2010

SUN	MON	TUES	WED	THUR	FRI	SAT
					1	2
3	4	5	6	7	8	9
10	11	12	13	14	15	16
17	18	19	20	21	22	23
24/31	25	26	27	28	29	30

APRIL – 2011

SUN	MON	TUES	WED	THUR	FRI	SAT
					1	2
3	4	5	6	7	8	9
10	11	12	13	14	15	16
17	18	19	20	21	22	23
24	25	26	27	28	29	30

NOVEMBER – 2010

SUN	MON	TUES	WED	THUR	FRI	SAT
	1	2	3	4	5	6
7	8	9	10	11	12	13
14	15	16	17	18	19	20
21	22	23	24	25	26	27
28	29	30				

MAY – 2011

SUN	MON	TUES	WED	THUR	FRI	SAT
1	2	3	4	5	6	7
8	9	10	11	12	13	14
15	16	17	18	19	20	21
22	23	24	25	26	27	28
29	30	31				

DECEMBER – 2010

SUN	MON	TUES	WED	THUR	FRI	SAT
		1	2	3	4	
5	6	7	8	9	10	11
12	13	14	15	16	17	18
19	20	21	22	23	24	25
26	27	28	29	30	31	

JUNE – 2011

SUN	MON	TUES	WED	THUR	FRI	SAT
		1	2	3	4	
5	6	7	8	9	10	11
12	13	14	15	16	17	18
19	20	21	22	23	24	25
26	27	28	29	30		

2011-2012 School Year

JULY – 2011

SUN	MON	TUES	WED	THUR	FRI	SAT
					1	2
3	4	5	6	7	8	9
10	11	12	13	14	15	16
17	18	19	20	21	22	23
24/31	25	26	27	28	29	30

JANUARY – 2012

SUN	MON	TUES	WED	THUR	FRI	SAT
1	2	3	4	5	6	7
8	9	10	11	12	13	14
15	16	17	18	19	20	21
22	23	24	25	26	27	28
29	30	31				

AUGUST – 2011

SUN	MON	TUES	WED	THUR	FRI	SAT
	1	2	3	4	5	6
7	8	9	10	11	12	13
14	15	16	17	18	19	20
21	22	23	24	25	26	27
28	29	30	31			

FEBRUARY – 2012

SUN	MON	TUES	WED	THUR	FRI	SAT
			1	2	3	4
5	6	7	8	9	10	11
12	13	14	15	16	17	18
19	20	21	22	23	24	25
26	27	28	29			

SEPTEMBER– 2011

SUN	MON	TUES	WED	THUR	FRI	SAT
				1	2	3
4	5	6	7	8	9	10
11	12	13	14	15	16	17
18	19	20	21	22	23	24
25	26	27	28	29	30	

MARCH – 2012

SUN	MON	TUES	WED	THUR	FRI	SAT
				1	2	3
4	5	6	7	8	9	10
11	12	13	14	15	16	17
18	19	20	21	22	23	24
25	26	27	28	29	30	31

OCTOBER – 2011

SUN	MON	TUES	WED	THUR	FRI	SAT
						1
2	3	4	5	6	7	8
9	10	11	12	13	14	15
16	17	18	19	20	21	22
23/30	24/31	25	26	27	28	29

APRIL – 2012

SUN	MON	TUES	WED	THUR	FRI	SAT
1	2	3	4	5	6	7
8	9	10	11	12	13	8
15	16	17	18	19	20	15
22	23	24	25	26	27	22
29	30					

NOVEMBER – 2011

SUN	MON	TUES	WED	THUR	FRI	SAT
		1	2	3	4	5
6	7	8	9	10	11	12
13	14	15	16	17	18	19
20	21	22	23	24	25	26
27	28	29	30			

MAY – 2012

SUN	MON	TUES	WED	THUR	FRI	SAT
		1	2	3	4	5
6	7	8	9	10	11	12
13	14	15	16	17	18	19
20	21	22	23	24	25	26
27	28	29	30	31		

DECEMBER – 2011

SUN	MON	TUES	WED	THUR	FRI	SAT
				1	2	3
4	5	6	7	8	9	10
11	12	13	14	15	16	17
18	19	20	21	22	23	24
25	26	27	28	29	30	31

JUNE – 2012

SUN	MON	TUES	WED	THUR	FRI	SAT
					1	2
3	4	5	6	7	8	9
10	11	12	13	14	15	16
17	18	19	20	21	22	23
24	25	26	27	28	29	30

2012-2013 School Year

JULY – 2012

SUN	MON	TUES	WED	THUR	FRI	SAT
1	2	3	4	5	6	7
8	9	10	11	12	13	14
15	16	17	18	19	20	21
22	23	24	25	26	27	28
29	30	31				

JANUARY – 2013

SUN	MON	TUES	WED	THUR	FRI	SAT
		1	2	3	4	5
6	7	8	9	10	11	12
13	14	15	16	17	18	19
20	21	22	23	24	25	26
27	28	29	30	31		

AUGUST – 2012

SUN	MON	TUES	WED	THUR	FRI	SAT
			1	2	3	4
5	6	7	8	9	10	11
12	13	14	15	16	17	18
19	20	21	22	23	24	25
26	27	28	29	30	31	

FEBRUARY – 2013

SUN	MON	TUES	WED	THUR	FRI	SAT
					1	2
3	4	5	6	7	8	9
10	11	12	13	14	15	16
17	18	19	20	21	22	23
24	25	26	27	28		

SEPTEMBER – 2012

SUN	MON	TUES	WED	THUR	FRI	SAT
						1
2	3	4	5	6	7	8
9	10	11	12	13	14	15
16	17	18	19	20	21	22
23/30	24	25	26	27	28	29

MARCH – 2013

SUN	MON	TUES	WED	THUR	FRI	SAT
					1	2
3	4	5	6	7	8	9
10	11	12	13	14	15	16
17	18	19	20	21	22	23
24/31	25	26	27	28	29	30

OCTOBER – 2012

SUN	MON	TUES	WED	THUR	FRI	SAT
	1	2	3	4	5	6
7	8	9	10	11	12	13
14	15	16	17	18	19	20
21	22	23	24	25	26	27
28	29	30	31			

APRIL – 2013

SUN	MON	TUES	WED	THUR	FRI	SAT
	1	2	3	4	5	6
7	8	9	10	11	12	13
14	15	16	17	18	19	20
21	22	23	24	25	26	27
28	29	30				

NOVEMBER – 2012

SUN	MON	TUES	WED	THUR	FRI	SAT
				1	2	3
4	5	6	7	8	9	10
11	12	13	14	15	16	17
18	19	20	21	22	23	24
25	26	27	28	29	30	

MAY – 2013

SUN	MON	TUES	WED	THUR	FRI	SAT
			1	2	3	4
5	6	7	8	9	10	11
12	13	14	15	16	17	18
19	20	21	22	23	24	25
26	27	28	29	30	31	

DECEMBER – 2012

SUN	MON	TUES	WED	THUR	FRI	SAT
						1
2	3	4	5	6	7	8
9	10	11	12	13	14	15
16	17	18	19	20	21	22
23/30	24/31	25	26	27	28	29

JUNE – 2013

SUN	MON	TUES	WED	THUR	FRI	SAT
						1
2	3	4	5	6	7	8
9	10	11	12	13	14	15
16	17	18	19	20	21	22
23/30	24	25	26	27	28	29

2013 - 2014 School Year

JULY – 2013

SUN	MON	TUES	WED	THUR	FRI	SAT
	1	2	3	4	5	6
7	8	9	10	11	12	13
14	15	16	17	18	19	20
21	22	23	24	25	26	27
28	29	30	31			

JANUARY – 2014

SUN	MON	TUES	WED	THUR	FRI	SAT
			1	2	3	4
5	6	7	8	9	10	11
12	13	14	15	16	17	18
19	20	21	22	23	24	25
26	27	28	29	30	31	

AUGUST – 2013

SUN	MON	TUES	WED	THUR	FRI	SAT
				1	2	3
4	5	6	7	8	9	10
11	12	13	14	15	16	17
18	19	20	21	22	23	24
25	26	27	28	29	30	31

FEBRUARY – 2014

SUN	MON	TUES	WED	THUR	FRI	SAT
						1
2	3	4	5	6	7	8
9	10	11	12	13	14	15
16	17	18	19	20	21	22
23	24	25	26	27	28	

SEPTEMBER – 2013

SUN	MON	TUES	WED	THUR	FRI	SAT
1	2	3	4	5	6	7
8	9	10	11	12	13	8
15	16	17	18	19	20	15
22	23	24	25	26	27	22
29	30					

MARCH – 2014

SUN	MON	TUES	WED	THUR	FRI	SAT
						1
2	3	4	5	6	7	8
9	10	11	12	13	14	15
16	17	18	19	20	21	22
23/30	24/31	25	26	27	28	29

OCTOBER – 2013

SUN	MON	TUES	WED	THUR	FRI	SAT
		1	2	3	4	5
6	7	8	9	10	11	12
13	14	15	16	17	18	19
20	21	22	23	24	25	26
27	28	29	30	31		

APRIL – 2014

SUN	MON	TUES	WED	THUR	FRI	SAT
		1	2	3	4	5
6	7	8	9	10	11	12
13	14	15	16	17	18	19
20	21	22	23	24	25	26
27	28	29	30			

NOVEMBER – 2013

SUN	MON	TUES	WED	THUR	FRI	SAT
					1	2
3	4	5	6	7	8	9
10	11	12	13	14	15	16
17	18	19	20	21	22	23
24	25	26	27	28	29	30

MAY – 2014

SUN	MON	TUES	WED	THUR	FRI	SAT
				1	2	3
4	5	6	7	8	9	10
11	12	13	14	15	16	17
18	19	20	21	22	23	24
25	26	27	28	29	30	31

DECEMBER – 2013

SUN	MON	TUES	WED	THUR	FRI	SAT
1	2	3	4	5	6	7
8	9	10	11	12	13	8
15	16	17	18	19	20	15
22	23	24	25	26	27	22
29	30	31				

JUNE – 2014

SUN	MON	TUES	WED	THUR	FRI	SAT
1	2	3	4	5	6	7
8	9	10	11	12	13	8
15	16	17	18	19	20	15
22	23	24	25	26	27	22
29	30					

OBJECTIVES AND RESOURCES

	Estimated Hours

Go to the ant, thou sluggard; consider her ways and be wise, . . .she provideth her food in the summer and gathers her food in the harvest. Proverbs 6:6 -8

OBJECTIVES AND RESOURCES

	Estimated Hours

Trust the Lord with all thine heart and lean not unto thine own understanding.

In all way acknowledge Him and He shall direct your path. Prov. 3:5,6

Resource List

Title	Grade Level	Subject/Description	Cost

Trust the Lord with all thine heart and lean not unto thine own understanding. In all way acknowledge Him and He shall direct your path. Prov. 3:5,6

LENDING AND BORROWING RESOURCE LIST

DESCRIPTION		Ⓛ ENT TO OR Ⓑ ORROWED FROM	DATE RECEIVED	DATE RETURNED
	Ⓛ Ⓑ			
	Ⓛ Ⓑ			
	Ⓛ Ⓑ			
	Ⓛ Ⓑ			
	Ⓛ Ⓑ			
	Ⓛ Ⓑ			
	Ⓛ Ⓑ			
	Ⓛ Ⓑ			
	Ⓛ Ⓑ			
	Ⓛ Ⓑ			
	Ⓛ Ⓑ			
	Ⓛ Ⓑ			
	Ⓛ Ⓑ			
	Ⓛ Ⓑ			
	Ⓛ Ⓑ			
	Ⓛ Ⓑ			
	Ⓛ Ⓑ			
	Ⓛ Ⓑ			
	Ⓛ Ⓑ			
	Ⓛ Ⓑ			
	Ⓛ Ⓑ			
	Ⓛ Ⓑ			
	Ⓛ Ⓑ			
	Ⓛ Ⓑ			
	Ⓛ Ⓑ			
	Ⓛ Ⓑ			
	Ⓛ Ⓑ			
	Ⓛ Ⓑ			
	Ⓛ Ⓑ			
	Ⓛ Ⓑ			
	Ⓛ Ⓑ			
	Ⓛ Ⓑ			

Thine heart shall not be grieved when thou givest unto him, because for this thing
the Lord thy god shall bless thee in all thy works. . . Deut. 15:10

YEARLY REQUIREMENTS

SUBJECTS	FRESHMAN YEAR COURSE TITLE		SOPHOMORE YEAR COURSE TITLE		JUNIOR YEAR COURSE TITLE		SENIOR YEAR COURSE TITLE	
ENGLISH								
MATHEMATICS								
SCIENCE								
SOCIAL STUDIES								
ARTS AND HUMANITIES								
COMPUTER SCIENCE/ BUSINESS								
ELECTIVE AREAS								
ELECTIVE AREAS								
TOTAL CREDITS								

*CR-CREDIT. UNIT OF CREDIT IS 1=1Year, 1/2=1/2 Year

Yearly requirements vary from state to state. This chart is meant to be used as a guideline for recording the student's progress through their high school years. Most four year universities/colleges will minimally accept the following: four years of English, two years of advanced math; two to four years of history and social science; two to four years of laboratory science; two to four years of the same foreign language; one to two years of music and art; and computer skills. It is also important to document interests, activities, achievements, business skill (i.e. a home business), and volunteer work.

Evaluator: _____

Qualifications: _____

Address: _____

Phone: _____ Evaluation Date: _____

DAILY ATTENDANCE SUBJECTS GRADES

Date	Attendance	1	2	3	4	5	6	7	8	9	10	Date	Attendance	1	2	3	4	5	6	7	8	9	10
GRADE AVERAGE												GRADE AVERAGE											
GRADE AVERAGE												GRADE AVERAGE											
GRADE AVERAGE												GRADE AVERAGE											
GRADE AVERAGE												GRADE AVERAGE											

DAILY ATTENDANCE SUBJECTS GRADES

Date	Attendance	1	2	3	4	5	6	7	8	9	10	Date	Attendance	1	2	3	4	5	6	7	8	9	10
GRADE AVERAGE												GRADE AVERAGE											
GRADE AVERAGE												GRADE AVERAGE											
GRADE AVERAGE												GRADE AVERAGE											
GRADE AVERAGE												GRADE AVERAGE											
GRADE AVERAGE												GRADE AVERAGE											

DAILY ATTENDANCE SUBJECTS GRADES

Date	Attendance	1	2	3	4	5	6	7	8	9	10	Date	Attendance	1	2	3	4	5	6	7	8	9	10
GRADE AVERAGE												GRADE AVERAGE											
GRADE AVERAGE												GRADE AVERAGE											
GRADE AVERAGE												GRADE AVERAGE											
GRADE AVERAGE												GRADE AVERAGE											
GRADE AVERAGE												GRADE AVERAGE											

DAILY ATTENDANCE SUBJECTS GRADES

Date	Attendance	1	2	3	4	5	6	7	8	9	10	Date	Attendance	1	2	3	4	5	6	7	8	9	10
GRADE AVERAGE												GRADE AVERAGE											
GRADE AVERAGE												GRADE AVERAGE											
GRADE AVERAGE												GRADE AVERAGE											
GRADE AVERAGE												GRADE AVERAGE											

FIELD TRIP LOG

Field Trip To:	Host's Name
Objectives:	**Phone #**
	Date:

Field Trip To:	Host's Name
Objectives:	**Phone #**
	Date:

Field Trip To:	Host's Name
Objectives:	**Phone #**
	Date:

Field Trip To:	Host's Name
Objectives:	**Phone #**
	Date:

Field Trip To:	Host's Name
Objectives:	**Phone #**
	Date:

Field Trip To:	Host's Name
Objectives:	**Phone #**
	Date:

Field Trip To:	Host's Name
Objectives:	**Phone #**
	Date:

FIELD TRIP LOG

Field Trip To:

Host's Name

Objectives:

Phone #

Date:

Field Trip To:

Host's Name

Objectives:

Phone #

Date:

Field Trip To:

Host's Name

Objectives:

Phone #

Date:

Field Trip To:

Host's Name

Objectives:

Phone #

Date:

Field Trip To:

Host's Name

Objectives:

Phone #

Date:

Field Trip To:

Host's Name

Objectives:

Phone #

Date:

Field Trip To:

Host's Name

Objectives:

Phone #

Date:

___ Subject	___ Subject	___ Subject	Notes	Week #

___ Subject	___ Subject	___ Subject

___ Subject	___ Subject	___ Subject

Field Trips/Community Service

___ Subject	___ Subject	___ Subject

Subject #	Time in Quarter-hours	Weekly Total
___	⊕⊕⊕⊕⊕⊕	☐
___	⊕⊕⊕⊕⊕⊕	☐
___	⊕⊕⊕⊕⊕⊕	☐
___	⊕⊕⊕⊕⊕⊕	☐
___	⊕⊕⊕⊕⊕⊕	☐
___	⊕⊕⊕⊕⊕⊕	☐
___	⊕⊕⊕⊕⊕⊕	☐
___	⊕⊕⊕⊕⊕⊕	☐
___	⊕⊕⊕⊕⊕⊕	☐
___	⊕⊕⊕⊕⊕⊕	☐

___ Subject	___ Subject	___ Subject

S M T W T F S / Date	___ Subject	___ Subject	___ Subject	___ Subject
S M T W T F S / Date	___ Subject	___ Subject	___ Subject	___ Subject
S M T W T F S / Date	___ Subject	___ Subject	___ Subject	___ Subject
S M T W T F S / Date	___ Subject	___ Subject	___ Subject	___ Subject
S M T W T F S / Date	___ Subject	___ Subject	___ Subject	___ Subject

___ Subject	___ Subject	___ Subject

___ Subject	___ Subject	___ Subject

___ Subject	___ Subject	___ Subject

Field Trips/Community Service

___ Subject	___ Subject	___ Subject

Subject #	Time in Quarter-hours	Weekly Total
___	⊕⊕⊕⊕⊕⊕	☐
___	⊕⊕⊕⊕⊕⊕	☐
___	⊕⊕⊕⊕⊕⊕	☐
___	⊕⊕⊕⊕⊕⊕	☐
___	⊕⊕⊕⊕⊕⊕	☐
___	⊕⊕⊕⊕⊕⊕	☐
___	⊕⊕⊕⊕⊕⊕	☐
___	⊕⊕⊕⊕⊕⊕	☐
___	⊕⊕⊕⊕⊕⊕	☐
___	⊕⊕⊕⊕⊕⊕	☐

___ Subject	___ Subject	___ Subject

S	___ **Subject**	___ **Subject**	___ **Subject**	___ **Subject**
M				
T				
W				
T				
F				
S				
Date /				

S	___ **Subject**	___ **Subject**	___ **Subject**	___ **Subject**
M				
T				
W				
T				
F				
S				
Date /				

S	___ **Subject**	___ **Subject**	___ **Subject**	___ **Subject**
M				
T				
W				
T				
F				
S				
Date /				

S	___ **Subject**	___ **Subject**	___ **Subject**	___ **Subject**
M				
T				
W				
T				
F				
S				
Date /				

S	___ **Subject**	___ **Subject**	___ **Subject**	___ **Subject**
M				
T				
W				
T				
F				
S				
Date /				

___ Subject	___ Subject	___ Subject	Notes Week #
___ Subject	___ Subject	___ Subject	
___ Subject	___ Subject	___ Subject	Field Trips/Community Service
___ Subject	___ Subject	___ Subject	
___ Subject	___ Subject	___ Subject	

Subject #	Time in Quarter-hours	Weekly Total
___	⊕⊕⊕⊕⊕⊕	☐
___	⊕⊕⊕⊕⊕⊕	☐
___	⊕⊕⊕⊕⊕⊕	☐
___	⊕⊕⊕⊕⊕⊕	☐
___	⊕⊕⊕⊕⊕⊕	☐
___	⊕⊕⊕⊕⊕⊕	☐
___	⊕⊕⊕⊕⊕⊕	☐
___	⊕⊕⊕⊕⊕⊕	☐
___	⊕⊕⊕⊕⊕⊕	☐
___	⊕⊕⊕⊕⊕⊕	☐

	___ Subject	___ Subject	___ Subject	___ Subject
S				
M				
T				
W				
T				
F				
S				
Date /				

	___ Subject	___ Subject	___ Subject	___ Subject
S				
M				
T				
W				
T				
F				
S				
Date /				

	___ Subject	___ Subject	___ Subject	___ Subject
S				
M				
T				
W				
T				
F				
S				
Date /				

	___ Subject	___ Subject	___ Subject	___ Subject
S				
M				
T				
W				
T				
F				
S				
Date /				

	___ Subject	___ Subject	___ Subject	___ Subject
S				
M				
T				
W				
T				
F				
S				
Date /				

___ Subject	___ Subject	___ Subject	Notes	Week #

___ Subject	___ Subject	___ Subject

___ Subject	___ Subject	___ Subject

Field Trips/Community Service

___ Subject	___ Subject	___ Subject

Subject #	Time in Quarter-hours	Weekly Total

___ Subject	___ Subject	___ Subject

	___ Subject	___ Subject	___ Subject	___ Subject
S M T W T F S				
Date /				

	___ Subject	___ Subject	___ Subject	___ Subject
S M T W T F S				
Date /				

	___ Subject	___ Subject	___ Subject	___ Subject
S M T W T F S				
Date /				

	___ Subject	___ Subject	___ Subject	___ Subject
S M T W T F S				
Date /				

	___ Subject	___ Subject	___ Subject	___ Subject
S M T W T F S				
Date /				

___ **Subject**	___ **Subject**	___ **Subject**	**Notes**	**Week #** [4]

___ **Subject**	___ **Subject**	___ **Subject**

___ **Subject**	___ **Subject**	___ **Subject**

Field Trips/Community Service

___ **Subject**	___ **Subject**	___ **Subject**

___ **Subject**	___ **Subject**	___ **Subject**

Subject #	**Time in Quarter-hours**	**Weekly Total**
___	⊕⊕⊕⊕⊕⊕	☐
___	⊕⊕⊕⊕⊕⊕	☐
___	⊕⊕⊕⊕⊕⊕	☐
___	⊕⊕⊕⊕⊕⊕	☐
___	⊕⊕⊕⊕⊕⊕	☐
___	⊕⊕⊕⊕⊕⊕	☐
___	⊕⊕⊕⊕⊕⊕	☐
___	⊕⊕⊕⊕⊕⊕	☐
___	⊕⊕⊕⊕⊕⊕	☐
___	⊕⊕⊕⊕⊕⊕	☐

S	___ Subject	___ Subject	___ Subject	___ Subject
M				
T				
W				
T				
F				
S				
Date /				

S	___ Subject	___ Subject	___ Subject	___ Subject
M				
T				
W				
T				
F				
S				
Date /				

S	___ Subject	___ Subject	___ Subject	___ Subject
M				
T				
W				
T				
F				
S				
Date /				

S	___ Subject	___ Subject	___ Subject	___ Subject
M				
T				
W				
T				
F				
S				
Date /				

S	___ Subject	___ Subject	___ Subject	___ Subject
M				
T				
W				
T				
F				
S				
Date /				

___ Subject	___ Subject	___ Subject

___ Subject	___ Subject	___ Subject

___ Subject	___ Subject	___ Subject

___ Subject	___ Subject	___ Subject

___ Subject	___ Subject	___ Subject

Notes

Field Trips/Community Service

Subject #	Time in Quarter-hours	Weekly Total

S	___ **Subject**	___ **Subject**	___ **Subject**	___ **Subject**
M				
T				
W				
T				
F				
S				
Date /				

S	___ **Subject**	___ **Subject**	___ **Subject**	___ **Subject**
M				
T				
W				
T				
F				
S				
Date /				

S	___ **Subject**	___ **Subject**	___ **Subject**	___ **Subject**
M				
T				
W				
T				
F				
S				
Date /				

S	___ **Subject**	___ **Subject**	___ **Subject**	___ **Subject**
M				
T				
W				
T				
F				
S				
Date /				

S	___ **Subject**	___ **Subject**	___ **Subject**	___ **Subject**
M				
T				
W				
T				
F				
S				
Date /				

___ Subject	___ Subject	___ Subject	Notes	Week #

___ Subject	___ Subject	___ Subject

___ Subject	___ Subject	___ Subject

Field Trips/Community Service

___ Subject	___ Subject	___ Subject

Subject #	Time in Quarter-hours	Weekly Total

___ Subject	___ Subject	___ Subject

S	___ Subject	___ Subject	___ Subject	___ Subject
M				
T				
W				
T				
F				
S				
Date /				

S	___ Subject	___ Subject	___ Subject	___ Subject
M				
T				
W				
T				
F				
S				
Date /				

S	___ Subject	___ Subject	___ Subject	___ Subject
M				
T				
W				
T				
F				
S				
Date /				

S	___ Subject	___ Subject	___ Subject	___ Subject
M				
T				
W				
T				
F				
S				
Date /				

S	___ Subject	___ Subject	___ Subject	___ Subject
M				
T				
W				
T				
F				
S				
Date /				

___ **Subject**	___ **Subject**	___ **Subject**	**Notes**	**Week #** 7

___ **Subject**	___ **Subject**	___ **Subject**

___ **Subject**	___ **Subject**	___ **Subject**

Field Trips/Community Service

___ **Subject**	___ **Subject**	___ **Subject**

Subject #	**Time in Quarter-hours**	**Weekly Total**

___ **Subject**	___ **Subject**	___ **Subject**

S	___ **Subject**	___ **Subject**	___ **Subject**	___ **Subject**
M				
T				
W				
T				
F				
S				
Date /				

S	___ **Subject**	___ **Subject**	___ **Subject**	___ **Subject**
M				
T				
W				
T				
F				
S				
Date /				

S	___ **Subject**	___ **Subject**	___ **Subject**	___ **Subject**
M				
T				
W				
T				
F				
S				
Date /				

S	___ **Subject**	___ **Subject**	___ **Subject**	___ **Subject**
M				
T				
W				
T				
F				
S				
Date /				

S	___ **Subject**	___ **Subject**	___ **Subject**	___ **Subject**
M				
T				
W				
T				
F				
S				
Date /				

___ Subject	___ Subject	___ Subject	Notes	Week #

___ Subject	___ Subject	___ Subject

___ Subject	___ Subject	___ Subject

Field Trips/Community Service

___ Subject	___ Subject	___ Subject

___ Subject	___ Subject	___ Subject

Subject #	Time in Quarter-hours	Weekly Total

S	___ Subject	___ Subject	___ Subject	___ Subject
M				
T				
W				
T				
F				
S				
Date /				

S	___ Subject	___ Subject	___ Subject	___ Subject
M				
T				
W				
T				
F				
S				
Date /				

S	___ Subject	___ Subject	___ Subject	___ Subject
M				
T				
W				
T				
F				
S				
Date /				

S	___ Subject	___ Subject	___ Subject	___ Subject
M				
T				
W				
T				
F				
S				
Date /				

S	___ Subject	___ Subject	___ Subject	___ Subject
M				
T				
W				
T				
F				
S				
Date /				

___ **Subject**	___ **Subject**	___ **Subject**	**Notes**	**Week #**

___ **Subject**	___ **Subject**	___ **Subject**

___ **Subject**	___ **Subject**	___ **Subject**

Field Trips/Community Service

___ **Subject**	___ **Subject**	___ **Subject**

Subject #	**Time in Quarter-hours**	**Weekly Total**
___	⊕⊕⊕⊕⊕⊕	☐
___	⊕⊕⊕⊕⊕⊕	☐
___	⊕⊕⊕⊕⊕⊕	☐
___	⊕⊕⊕⊕⊕⊕	☐
___	⊕⊕⊕⊕⊕⊕	☐
___	⊕⊕⊕⊕⊕⊕	☐
___	⊕⊕⊕⊕⊕⊕	☐
___	⊕⊕⊕⊕⊕⊕	☐
___	⊕⊕⊕⊕⊕⊕	☐
___	⊕⊕⊕⊕⊕⊕	☐

___ **Subject**	___ **Subject**	___ **Subject**

S	___ Subject	___ Subject	___ Subject	___ Subject
M				
T				
W				
T				
F				
S				
Date /				

S	___ Subject	___ Subject	___ Subject	___ Subject
M				
T				
W				
T				
F				
S				
Date /				

S	___ Subject	___ Subject	___ Subject	___ Subject
M				
T				
W				
T				
F				
S				
Date /				

S	___ Subject	___ Subject	___ Subject	___ Subject
M				
T				
W				
T				
F				
S				
Date /				

S	___ Subject	___ Subject	___ Subject	___ Subject
M				
T				
W				
T				
F				
S				
Date /				

___ **Subject**	___ **Subject**	___ **Subject**	**Notes**	**Week #**

___ **Subject**	___ **Subject**	___ **Subject**

___ **Subject**	___ **Subject**	___ **Subject**

Field Trips/Community Service

___ **Subject**	___ **Subject**	___ **Subject**

Subject #	**Time in Quarter-hours**	**Weekly Total**

___ **Subject**	___ **Subject**	___ **Subject**

S	___ **Subject**	___ **Subject**	___ **Subject**	___ **Subject**
M				
T				
W				
T				
F				
S				
Date				
/				

S	___ **Subject**	___ **Subject**	___ **Subject**	___ **Subject**
M				
T				
W				
T				
F				
S				
Date				
/				

S	___ **Subject**	___ **Subject**	___ **Subject**	___ **Subject**
M				
T				
W				
T				
F				
S				
Date				
/				

S	___ **Subject**	___ **Subject**	___ **Subject**	___ **Subject**
M				
T				
W				
T				
F				
S				
Date				
/				

S	___ **Subject**	___ **Subject**	___ **Subject**	___ **Subject**
M				
T				
W				
T				
F				
S				
Date				
/				

___ Subject	___ Subject	___ Subject

Notes   **Week #** ☐

Field Trips/Community Service

Subject #	Time in Quarter-hours	Weekly Total
___	⊕⊕⊕⊕⊕⊕	☐
___	⊕⊕⊕⊕⊕⊕	☐
___	⊕⊕⊕⊕⊕⊕	☐
___	⊕⊕⊕⊕⊕⊕	☐
___	⊕⊕⊕⊕⊕⊕	☐
___	⊕⊕⊕⊕⊕⊕	☐
___	⊕⊕⊕⊕⊕⊕	☐
___	⊕⊕⊕⊕⊕⊕	☐
___	⊕⊕⊕⊕⊕⊕	☐
___	⊕⊕⊕⊕⊕⊕	☐

___ Subject	___ Subject	___ Subject

___ Subject	___ Subject	___ Subject

___ Subject	___ Subject	___ Subject

___ Subject	___ Subject	___ Subject

	___ Subject	___ Subject	___ Subject	___ Subject
S M T W T F S				
Date /				

	___ Subject	___ Subject	___ Subject	___ Subject
S M T W T F S				
Date /				

	___ Subject	___ Subject	___ Subject	___ Subject
S M T W T F S				
Date /				

	___ Subject	___ Subject	___ Subject	___ Subject
S M T W T F S				
Date /				

	___ Subject	___ Subject	___ Subject	___ Subject
S M T W T F S				
Date /				

___ Subject	___ Subject	___ Subject	Notes	Week #

___ Subject	___ Subject	___ Subject

___ Subject	___ Subject	___ Subject

Field Trips/Community Service

___ Subject	___ Subject	___ Subject

___ Subject	___ Subject	___ Subject

Subject #	Time in Quarter-hours	Weekly Total

S	___ **Subject**	___ **Subject**	___ **Subject**	___ **Subject**
M				
T				
W				
T				
F				
S				
Date /				

S	___ **Subject**	___ **Subject**	___ **Subject**	___ **Subject**
M				
T				
W				
T				
F				
S				
Date /				

S	___ **Subject**	___ **Subject**	___ **Subject**	___ **Subject**
M				
T				
W				
T				
F				
S				
Date /				

S	___ **Subject**	___ **Subject**	___ **Subject**	___ **Subject**
M				
T				
W				
T				
F				
S				
Date /				

S	___ **Subject**	___ **Subject**	___ **Subject**	___ **Subject**
M				
T				
W				
T				
F				
S				
Date /				

___ Subject	___ Subject	___ Subject	Notes Week #
___ Subject	___ Subject	___ Subject	
___ Subject	___ Subject	___ Subject	Field Trips/Community Service

___ Subject	___ Subject	___ Subject

___ Subject	___ Subject	___ Subject

Subject #	Time in Quarter-hours	Weekly Total
___	⊕⊕⊕⊕⊕⊕	☐
___	⊕⊕⊕⊕⊕⊕	☐
___	⊕⊕⊕⊕⊕⊕	☐
___	⊕⊕⊕⊕⊕⊕	☐
___	⊕⊕⊕⊕⊕⊕	☐
___	⊕⊕⊕⊕⊕⊕	☐
___	⊕⊕⊕⊕⊕⊕	☐
___	⊕⊕⊕⊕⊕⊕	☐
___	⊕⊕⊕⊕⊕⊕	☐
___	⊕⊕⊕⊕⊕⊕	☐

S	___ Subject	___ Subject	___ Subject	___ Subject
M				
T				
W				
T				
F				
S				
Date /				

S	___ Subject	___ Subject	___ Subject	___ Subject
M				
T				
W				
T				
F				
S				
Date /				

S	___ Subject	___ Subject	___ Subject	___ Subject
M				
T				
W				
T				
F				
S				
Date /				

S	___ Subject	___ Subject	___ Subject	___ Subject
M				
T				
W				
T				
F				
S				
Date /				

S	___ Subject	___ Subject	___ Subject	___ Subject
M				
T				
W				
T				
F				
S				
Date /				

___ Subject	___ Subject	___ Subject	Notes	Week #

___ Subject	___ Subject	___ Subject

___ Subject	___ Subject	___ Subject

Field Trips/Community Service

___ Subject	___ Subject	___ Subject

___ Subject	___ Subject	___ Subject

Subject #	Time in Quarter-hours	Weekly Total

S	___ **Subject**	___ **Subject**	___ **Subject**	___ **Subject**
M				
T				
W				
T				
F				
S				
Date /				

S	___ **Subject**	___ **Subject**	___ **Subject**	___ **Subject**
M				
T				
W				
T				
F				
S				
Date /				

S	___ **Subject**	___ **Subject**	___ **Subject**	___ **Subject**
M				
T				
W				
T				
F				
S				
Date /				

S	___ **Subject**	___ **Subject**	___ **Subject**	___ **Subject**
M				
T				
W				
T				
F				
S				
Date /				

S	___ **Subject**	___ **Subject**	___ **Subject**	___ **Subject**
M				
T				
W				
T				
F				
S				
Date /				

___ Subject	___ Subject	___ Subject	Notes	Week #
___ Subject	___ Subject	___ Subject		
___ Subject	___ Subject	___ Subject	Field Trips/Community Service	
___ Subject	___ Subject	___ Subject		
___ Subject	___ Subject	___ Subject		

Subject #	Time in Quarter-hours	Weekly Total
___	⊕⊕⊕⊕⊕⊕	☐
___	⊕⊕⊕⊕⊕⊕	☐
___	⊕⊕⊕⊕⊕⊕	☐
___	⊕⊕⊕⊕⊕⊕	☐
___	⊕⊕⊕⊕⊕⊕	☐
___	⊕⊕⊕⊕⊕⊕	☐
___	⊕⊕⊕⊕⊕⊕	☐
___	⊕⊕⊕⊕⊕⊕	☐
___	⊕⊕⊕⊕⊕⊕	☐
___	⊕⊕⊕⊕⊕⊕	☐

S	___ Subject	___ Subject	___ Subject	___ Subject
M				
T				
W				
T				
F				
S				
Date /				

S	___ Subject	___ Subject	___ Subject	___ Subject
M				
T				
W				
T				
F				
S				
Date /				

S	___ Subject	___ Subject	___ Subject	___ Subject
M				
T				
W				
T				
F				
S				
Date /				

S	___ Subject	___ Subject	___ Subject	___ Subject
M				
T				
W				
T				
F				
S				
Date /				

S	___ Subject	___ Subject	___ Subject	___ Subject
M				
T				
W				
T				
F				
S				
Date /				

___ Subject	___ Subject	___ Subject	Notes	Week #

___ Subject	___ Subject	___ Subject

___ Subject	___ Subject	___ Subject

Field Trips/Community Service

___ Subject	___ Subject	___ Subject

___ Subject	___ Subject	___ Subject

Subject #	Time in Quarter-hours	Weekly Total
___	⊕⊕⊕⊕⊕⊕	☐
___	⊕⊕⊕⊕⊕⊕	☐
___	⊕⊕⊕⊕⊕⊕	☐
___	⊕⊕⊕⊕⊕⊕	☐
___	⊕⊕⊕⊕⊕⊕	☐
___	⊕⊕⊕⊕⊕⊕	☐
___	⊕⊕⊕⊕⊕⊕	☐
___	⊕⊕⊕⊕⊕⊕	☐
___	⊕⊕⊕⊕⊕⊕	☐
___	⊕⊕⊕⊕⊕⊕	☐

	___ **Subject**	___ **Subject**	___ **Subject**	___ **Subject**
S				
M				
T				
W				
T				
F				
S				
Date /				

	___ **Subject**	___ **Subject**	___ **Subject**	___ **Subject**
S				
M				
T				
W				
T				
F				
S				
Date /				

	___ **Subject**	___ **Subject**	___ **Subject**	___ **Subject**
S				
M				
T				
W				
T				
F				
S				
Date /				

	___ **Subject**	___ **Subject**	___ **Subject**	___ **Subject**
S				
M				
T				
W				
T				
F				
S				
Date /				

	___ **Subject**	___ **Subject**	___ **Subject**	___ **Subject**
S				
M				
T				
W				
T				
F				
S				
Date /				

____ Subject	____ Subject	____ Subject	Notes	Week #

____ Subject	____ Subject	____ Subject

____ Subject	____ Subject	____ Subject

Field Trips/Community Service

____ Subject	____ Subject	____ Subject

____ Subject	____ Subject	____ Subject

Subject #	Time in Quarter-hours	Weekly Total
___	⊕⊕⊕⊕⊕⊕	☐
___	⊕⊕⊕⊕⊕⊕	☐
___	⊕⊕⊕⊕⊕⊕	☐
___	⊕⊕⊕⊕⊕⊕	☐
___	⊕⊕⊕⊕⊕⊕	☐
___	⊕⊕⊕⊕⊕⊕	☐
___	⊕⊕⊕⊕⊕⊕	☐
___	⊕⊕⊕⊕⊕⊕	☐
___	⊕⊕⊕⊕⊕⊕	☐
___	⊕⊕⊕⊕⊕⊕	☐

S	___ **Subject**	___ **Subject**	___ **Subject**	___ **Subject**
M				
T				
W				
T				
F				
S				
Date /				

S	___ **Subject**	___ **Subject**	___ **Subject**	___ **Subject**
M				
T				
W				
T				
F				
S				
Date /				

S	___ **Subject**	___ **Subject**	___ **Subject**	___ **Subject**
M				
T				
W				
T				
F				
S				
Date /				

S	___ **Subject**	___ **Subject**	___ **Subject**	___ **Subject**
M				
T				
W				
T				
F				
S				
Date /				

S	___ **Subject**	___ **Subject**	___ **Subject**	___ **Subject**
M				
T				
W				
T				
F				
S				
Date /				

___ Subject	___ Subject	___ Subject

Notes

Week #

___ Subject	___ Subject	___ Subject

___ Subject	___ Subject	___ Subject

Field Trips/Community Service

___ Subject	___ Subject	___ Subject

Subject #	Time in Quarter-hours	Weekly Total
___	⊕⊕⊕⊕⊕⊕	☐
___	⊕⊕⊕⊕⊕⊕	☐
___	⊕⊕⊕⊕⊕⊕	☐
___	⊕⊕⊕⊕⊕⊕	☐
___	⊕⊕⊕⊕⊕⊕	☐
___	⊕⊕⊕⊕⊕⊕	☐
___	⊕⊕⊕⊕⊕⊕	☐
___	⊕⊕⊕⊕⊕⊕	☐
___	⊕⊕⊕⊕⊕⊕	☐
___	⊕⊕⊕⊕⊕⊕	☐

___ Subject	___ Subject	___ Subject

	___ **Subject**	___ **Subject**	___ **Subject**	___ **Subject**
S				
M				
T				
W				
T				
F				
S				
Date /				

	___ **Subject**	___ **Subject**	___ **Subject**	___ **Subject**
S				
M				
T				
W				
T				
F				
S				
Date /				

	___ **Subject**	___ **Subject**	___ **Subject**	___ **Subject**
S				
M				
T				
W				
T				
F				
S				
Date /				

	___ **Subject**	___ **Subject**	___ **Subject**	___ **Subject**
S				
M				
T				
W				
T				
F				
S				
Date /				

	___ **Subject**	___ **Subject**	___ **Subject**	___ **Subject**
S				
M				
T				
W				
T				
F				
S				
Date /				

_____ Subject	_____ Subject	_____ Subject	Notes	Week #

_____ Subject	_____ Subject	_____ Subject

_____ Subject	_____ Subject	_____ Subject

Field Trips/Community Service

_____ Subject	_____ Subject	_____ Subject

_____ Subject	_____ Subject	_____ Subject

Subject #	Time in Quarter-hours	Weekly Total
___	⊕⊕⊕⊕⊕⊕	☐
___	⊕⊕⊕⊕⊕⊕	☐
___	⊕⊕⊕⊕⊕⊕	☐
___	⊕⊕⊕⊕⊕⊕	☐
___	⊕⊕⊕⊕⊕⊕	☐
___	⊕⊕⊕⊕⊕⊕	☐
___	⊕⊕⊕⊕⊕⊕	☐
___	⊕⊕⊕⊕⊕⊕	☐
___	⊕⊕⊕⊕⊕⊕	☐
___	⊕⊕⊕⊕⊕⊕	☐

S	___ Subject	___ Subject	___ Subject	___ Subject
M				
T				
W				
T				
F				
S				
Date /				

S	___ Subject	___ Subject	___ Subject	___ Subject
M				
T				
W				
T				
F				
S				
Date /				

S	___ Subject	___ Subject	___ Subject	___ Subject
M				
T				
W				
T				
F				
S				
Date /				

S	___ Subject	___ Subject	___ Subject	___ Subject
M				
T				
W				
T				
F				
S				
Date /				

S	___ Subject	___ Subject	___ Subject	___ Subject
M				
T				
W				
T				
F				
S				
Date /				

___ Subject	___ Subject	___ Subject

___ Subject	___ Subject	___ Subject

___ Subject	___ Subject	___ Subject

Field Trips/Community Service

___ Subject	___ Subject	___ Subject

Subject #	Time in Quarter-hours	Weekly Total

___ Subject	___ Subject	___ Subject

S	___ **Subject**	___ **Subject**	___ **Subject**	___ **Subject**
M				
T				
W				
T				
F				
S				
Date /				

S	___ **Subject**	___ **Subject**	___ **Subject**	___ **Subject**
M				
T				
W				
T				
F				
S				
Date /				

S	___ **Subject**	___ **Subject**	___ **Subject**	___ **Subject**
M				
T				
W				
T				
F				
S				
Date /				

S	___ **Subject**	___ **Subject**	___ **Subject**	___ **Subject**
M				
T				
W				
T				
F				
S				
Date /				

S	___ **Subject**	___ **Subject**	___ **Subject**	___ **Subject**
M				
T				
W				
T				
F				
S				
Date /				

_____ **Subject**	_____ **Subject**	_____ **Subject**

_____ **Subject**	_____ **Subject**	_____ **Subject**

_____ **Subject**	_____ **Subject**	_____ **Subject**

_____ **Subject**	_____ **Subject**	_____ **Subject**

_____ **Subject**	_____ **Subject**	_____ **Subject**

Notes   **Week #**

Field Trips/Community Service

Subject #	Time in Quarter-hours	Weekly Total

S	___ Subject	___ Subject	___ Subject	___ Subject
M				
T				
W				
T				
F				
S				
Date /				

S	___ Subject	___ Subject	___ Subject	___ Subject
M				
T				
W				
T				
F				
S				
Date /				

S	___ Subject	___ Subject	___ Subject	___ Subject
M				
T				
W				
T				
F				
S				
Date /				

S	___ Subject	___ Subject	___ Subject	___ Subject
M				
T				
W				
T				
F				
S				
Date /				

S	___ Subject	___ Subject	___ Subject	___ Subject
M				
T				
W				
T				
F				
S				
Date /				

___ Subject	___ Subject	___ Subject	Notes	Week #

___ Subject	___ Subject	___ Subject

___ Subject	___ Subject	___ Subject

Field Trips/Community Service

___ Subject	___ Subject	___ Subject

___ Subject	___ Subject	___ Subject

Subject #	Time in Quarter-hours	Weekly Total

	___ Subject	___ Subject	___ Subject	___ Subject
(S)(M)(T)(W)(T)(F)(S) Date /				
	___ Subject	___ Subject	___ Subject	___ Subject
(S)(M)(T)(W)(T)(F)(S) Date /				
	___ Subject	___ Subject	___ Subject	___ Subject
(S)(M)(T)(W)(T)(F)(S) Date /				
	___ Subject	___ Subject	___ Subject	___ Subject
(S)(M)(T)(W)(T)(F)(S) Date /				
	___ Subject	___ Subject	___ Subject	___ Subject
(S)(M)(T)(W)(T)(F)(S) Date /				

___ Subject	___ Subject	___ Subject	Notes	Week #

___ Subject	___ Subject	___ Subject

___ Subject	___ Subject	___ Subject

Field Trips/Community Service

___ Subject	___ Subject	___ Subject

Subject #	Time in Quarter-hours	Weekly Total

___ Subject	___ Subject	___ Subject

	___ Subject	___ Subject	___ Subject	___ Subject
S				
M				
T				
W				
T				
F				
S				
Date /				

	___ Subject	___ Subject	___ Subject	___ Subject
S				
M				
T				
W				
T				
F				
S				
Date /				

	___ Subject	___ Subject	___ Subject	___ Subject
S				
M				
T				
W				
T				
F				
S				
Date /				

	___ Subject	___ Subject	___ Subject	___ Subject
S				
M				
T				
W				
T				
F				
S				
Date /				

	___ Subject	___ Subject	___ Subject	___ Subject
S				
M				
T				
W				
T				
F				
S				
Date /				

___ Subject	___ Subject	___ Subject

Notes   **Week #** ☐

___ Subject	___ Subject	___ Subject

___ Subject	___ Subject	___ Subject

Field Trips/Community Service

___ Subject	___ Subject	___ Subject

Subject #	Time in Quarter-hours	Weekly Total
___	⊕⊕⊕⊕⊕⊕	☐
___	⊕⊕⊕⊕⊕⊕	☐
___	⊕⊕⊕⊕⊕⊕	☐
___	⊕⊕⊕⊕⊕⊕	☐
___	⊕⊕⊕⊕⊕⊕	☐
___	⊕⊕⊕⊕⊕⊕	☐
___	⊕⊕⊕⊕⊕⊕	☐
___	⊕⊕⊕⊕⊕⊕	☐
___	⊕⊕⊕⊕⊕⊕	☐
___	⊕⊕⊕⊕⊕⊕	☐

___ Subject	___ Subject	___ Subject

	___ Subject	___ Subject	___ Subject	___ Subject
S				
M				
T				
W				
T				
F				
S				
Date /				

	___ Subject	___ Subject	___ Subject	___ Subject
S				
M				
T				
W				
T				
F				
S				
Date /				

	___ Subject	___ Subject	___ Subject	___ Subject
S				
M				
T				
W				
T				
F				
S				
Date /				

	___ Subject	___ Subject	___ Subject	___ Subject
S				
M				
T				
W				
T				
F				
S				
Date /				

	___ Subject	___ Subject	___ Subject	___ Subject
S				
M				
T				
W				
T				
F				
S				
Date /				

___ Subject	___ Subject	___ Subject	Notes	Week #

___ Subject	___ Subject	___ Subject

___ Subject	___ Subject	___ Subject

Field Trips/Community Service

___ Subject	___ Subject	___ Subject

Subject #	Time in Quarter-hours	Weekly Total

___ Subject	___ Subject	___ Subject

	___ Subject	___ Subject	___ Subject	___ Subject
S				
M				
T				
W				
T				
F				
S				
Date /				

	___ Subject	___ Subject	___ Subject	___ Subject
S				
M				
T				
W				
T				
F				
S				
Date /				

	___ Subject	___ Subject	___ Subject	___ Subject
S				
M				
T				
W				
T				
F				
S				
Date /				

	___ Subject	___ Subject	___ Subject	___ Subject
S				
M				
T				
W				
T				
F				
S				
Date /				

	___ Subject	___ Subject	___ Subject	___ Subject
S				
M				
T				
W				
T				
F				
S				
Date /				

___ Subject	___ Subject	___ Subject	Notes	Week #

___ Subject	___ Subject	___ Subject

___ Subject	___ Subject	___ Subject

Field Trips/Community Service

___ Subject	___ Subject	___ Subject

___ Subject	___ Subject	___ Subject

Subject #	Time in Quarter-hours	Weekly Total

	___ Subject	___ Subject	___ Subject	___ Subject
S				
M				
T				
W				
T				
F				
S				
Date /				

	___ Subject	___ Subject	___ Subject	___ Subject
S				
M				
T				
W				
T				
F				
S				
Date /				

	___ Subject	___ Subject	___ Subject	___ Subject
S				
M				
T				
W				
T				
F				
S				
Date /				

	___ Subject	___ Subject	___ Subject	___ Subject
S				
M				
T				
W				
T				
F				
S				
Date /				

	___ Subject	___ Subject	___ Subject	___ Subject
S				
M				
T				
W				
T				
F				
S				
Date /				

___ Subject	___ Subject	___ Subject	Notes	Week #
___ Subject	___ Subject	___ Subject		
___ Subject	___ Subject	___ Subject	Field Trips/Community Service	
___ Subject	___ Subject	___ Subject		
___ Subject	___ Subject	___ Subject		

Subject #	Time in Quarter-hours	Weekly Total

S	___ Subject	___ Subject	___ Subject	___ Subject
M				
T				
W				
T				
F				
S				
Date /				

S	___ Subject	___ Subject	___ Subject	___ Subject
M				
T				
W				
T				
F				
S				
Date /				

S	___ Subject	___ Subject	___ Subject	___ Subject
M				
T				
W				
T				
F				
S				
Date /				

S	___ Subject	___ Subject	___ Subject	___ Subject
M				
T				
W				
T				
F				
S				
Date /				

S	___ Subject	___ Subject	___ Subject	___ Subject
M				
T				
W				
T				
F				
S				
Date /				

___ Subject	___ Subject	___ Subject	Notes	Week #

___ Subject	___ Subject	___ Subject

___ Subject	___ Subject	___ Subject

Field Trips/Community Service

___ Subject	___ Subject	___ Subject

Subject #	Time in Quarter-hours	Weekly Total

___ Subject	___ Subject	___ Subject

(S)	___ **Subject**	___ **Subject**	___ **Subject**	___ **Subject**
(M)				
(T)				
(W)				
(T)				
(F)				
(S)				
Date /				

(S)	___ **Subject**	___ **Subject**	___ **Subject**	___ **Subject**
(M)				
(T)				
(W)				
(T)				
(F)				
(S)				
Date /				

(S)	___ **Subject**	___ **Subject**	___ **Subject**	___ **Subject**
(M)				
(T)				
(W)				
(T)				
(F)				
(S)				
Date /				

(S)	___ **Subject**	___ **Subject**	___ **Subject**	___ **Subject**
(M)				
(T)				
(W)				
(T)				
(F)				
(S)				
Date /				

(S)	___ **Subject**	___ **Subject**	___ **Subject**	___ **Subject**
(M)				
(T)				
(W)				
(T)				
(F)				
(S)				
Date /				

___ Subject	___ Subject	___ Subject	Notes	Week #

___ Subject	___ Subject	___ Subject

___ Subject	___ Subject	___ Subject

Field Trips/Community Service

___ Subject	___ Subject	___ Subject

Subject #	Time in Quarter-hours	Weekly Total

___ Subject	___ Subject	___ Subject

S	___ **Subject**	___ **Subject**	___ **Subject**	___ **Subject**
M				
T				
W				
T				
F				
S				
Date /				

S	___ **Subject**	___ **Subject**	___ **Subject**	___ **Subject**
M				
T				
W				
T				
F				
S				
Date /				

S	___ **Subject**	___ **Subject**	___ **Subject**	___ **Subject**
M				
T				
W				
T				
F				
S				
Date /				

S	___ **Subject**	___ **Subject**	___ **Subject**	___ **Subject**
M				
T				
W				
T				
F				
S				
Date /				

S	___ **Subject**	___ **Subject**	___ **Subject**	___ **Subject**
M				
T				
W				
T				
F				
S				
Date /				

___ Subject	___ Subject	___ Subject	Notes	Week #

___ Subject	___ Subject	___ Subject

___ Subject	___ Subject	___ Subject

Field Trips/Community Service

___ Subject	___ Subject	___ Subject

Subject #	Time in Quarter-hours	Weekly Total
___	⊕⊕⊕⊕⊕⊕	☐
___	⊕⊕⊕⊕⊕⊕	☐
___	⊕⊕⊕⊕⊕⊕	☐
___	⊕⊕⊕⊕⊕⊕	☐
___	⊕⊕⊕⊕⊕⊕	☐
___	⊕⊕⊕⊕⊕⊕	☐
___	⊕⊕⊕⊕⊕⊕	☐
___	⊕⊕⊕⊕⊕⊕	☐
___	⊕⊕⊕⊕⊕⊕	☐
___	⊕⊕⊕⊕⊕⊕	☐

___ Subject	___ Subject	___ Subject

S	Subject	Subject	Subject	Subject
M				
T				
W				
T				
F				
S				
Date /				

S	Subject	Subject	Subject	Subject
M				
T				
W				
T				
F				
S				
Date /				

S	Subject	Subject	Subject	Subject
M				
T				
W				
T				
F				
S				
Date /				

S	Subject	Subject	Subject	Subject
M				
T				
W				
T				
F				
S				
Date /				

S	Subject	Subject	Subject	Subject
M				
T				
W				
T				
F				
S				
Date /				

___ **Subject**	___ **Subject**	___ **Subject**

___ **Subject**	___ **Subject**	___ **Subject**

___ **Subject**	___ **Subject**	___ **Subject**

___ **Subject**	___ **Subject**	___ **Subject**

___ **Subject**	___ **Subject**	___ **Subject**

Notes **Week #** ___

Field Trips/Community Service

Subject #	Time in Quarter-hours	Weekly Total
___	⊕⊕⊕⊕⊕⊕	☐
___	⊕⊕⊕⊕⊕⊕	☐
___	⊕⊕⊕⊕⊕⊕	☐
___	⊕⊕⊕⊕⊕⊕	☐
___	⊕⊕⊕⊕⊕⊕	☐
___	⊕⊕⊕⊕⊕⊕	☐
___	⊕⊕⊕⊕⊕⊕	☐
___	⊕⊕⊕⊕⊕⊕	☐
___	⊕⊕⊕⊕⊕⊕	☐
___	⊕⊕⊕⊕⊕⊕	☐

	___ Subject	___ Subject	___ Subject	___ Subject
S				
M				
T				
W				
T				
F				
S				
Date /				

	___ Subject	___ Subject	___ Subject	___ Subject
S				
M				
T				
W				
T				
F				
S				
Date /				

	___ Subject	___ Subject	___ Subject	___ Subject
S				
M				
T				
W				
T				
F				
S				
Date /				

	___ Subject	___ Subject	___ Subject	___ Subject
S				
M				
T				
W				
T				
F				
S				
Date /				

	___ Subject	___ Subject	___ Subject	___ Subject
S				
M				
T				
W				
T				
F				
S				
Date /				

___ Subject	___ Subject	___ Subject	Notes	Week #

___ Subject	___ Subject	___ Subject

___ Subject	___ Subject	___ Subject

Field Trips/Community Service

___ Subject	___ Subject	___ Subject

Subject #	Time in Quarter-hours	Weekly Total

___ Subject	___ Subject	___ Subject

Educational Supplements

Date/s	Title / Web Site Address	Author / Composer	Date Due	Classification									
				Book	Audio	Video	Music	Internet	Non-Fiction	Fiction	Biography	Reference	

EDUCATIONAL SUPPLEMENTS

DATE/S	TITLE / WEB SITE ADDRESS	AUTHOR / COMPOSER	DATE DUE	Classification								
				Book	Audio	Video	Music	Internet	Non-fiction	Fiction	Biography	Reference

Educational Supplements

Date/s	Title / Web Site Address	Author / Composer	Date Due	Classification								
				Book	Audio	Video	Music	Internet	Non-Fiction	Fiction	Biography	Reference

EDUCATIONAL SUPPLEMENTS

DATE/S	TITLE / WEB SITE ADDRESS	AUTHOR / COMPOSER	DATE DUE	Classification								
				BOOK	AUDIO	VIDEO	MUSIC	INTERNET	NON-FICTION	FICTION	BIOGRAPHY	REFERENCE

EDUCATIONAL SUPPLEMENTS

DATE/S	TITLE / WEB SITE ADDRESS	AUTHOR / COMPOSER	DATE DUE	Classification										
				BOOK	AUDIO	VIDEO	MUSIC	INTERNET	NON-FICTION	FICTION	BIOGRAPHY	REFERENCE

EDUCATIONAL SUPPLEMENTS

DATE/S	TITLE / WEB SITE ADDRESS	AUTHOR / COMPOSER	DATE DUE	Classification								
				BOOK	AUDIO	VIDEO	MUSIC	INTERNET	NON-FICTION	FICTION	BIOGRAPHY	REFERENCE

EDUCATIONAL SUPPLEMENTS

DATE/S	TITLE / WEB SITE ADDRESS	AUTHOR / COMPOSER	DATE DUE	Classification									
				BOOK	AUDIO	VIDEO	MUSIC	INTERNET	NON-FICTION	FICTION	BIOGRAPHY	REFERENCE	

Educational Supplements

DATE/S	TITLE / WEB SITE ADDRESS	AUTHOR / COMPOSER	DATE DUE	Classification								
				BOOK	AUDIO	VIDEO	MUSIC	INTERNET	NON-FICTION	FICTION	BIOGRAPHY	REFERENCE

Educational Supplements

Date/s	Title / Web Site Address	Author / Composer	Date Due	Classification										
				Book	Audio	Video	Music	Internet	Non-fiction	Fiction	Biography	Reference

Contacts

Name	Address	Phone #	E-mail

Contacts

Name	Address	Phone #	E-mail

NOTES

NOTES